Larry Page
And
Sergey Brin

A Biography of the Secretive Google Billionaires

By
Austin Mathis

© Copyright 2019 - All rights reserved.

The content contained within this book may not be reproduced, duplicated or transmitted without direct written permission from the author or the publisher.

Under no circumstances will any blame or legal responsibility be held against the publisher, or author, for any damages, reparation, or monetary loss due to the information contained within this book, either directly or indirectly.

Legal Notice:

This book is copyright protected. It is only for personal use. You cannot amend, distribute, sell, use, quote or paraphrase any part, or the content within this book, without the consent of the author or publisher.

Disclaimer Notice:

Please note the information contained within this document is for educational and entertainment purposes only. All effort has been executed to present accurate, up to date, reliable, complete information. No warranties of any kind are declared or implied. Readers acknowledge that the author is not engaging in the rendering of legal, financial, medical or professional advice. The content within this book has been derived from various sources. Please consult a licensed professional before attempting any techniques outlined in this book.

By reading this document, the reader agrees that under no circumstances is the author responsible for any losses, direct or indirect, that are incurred as a result of the use of the information contained within this document, including, but not limited to, errors, omissions, or inaccuracies.

Table of Contents

Introduction _____ 5

Larry's Early Life _____ 8

Sergey's Early Life _____ 14

A New Friendship _____ 18

Growing Pains for Google _____ 27

The Early Authority of Google, Inc. ____ 35

The IPO of Google _____ 44

Continued Growth and a New CEO ____ 52

Google in 2012 and Beyond _____ 64

A New Era for Google _____ 72

Legal Issues for Google _____ 77

The Current Social Responsibility of Google _____ 81

References _____ 84

Introduction

Called the greatest development of the 20th century, the internet has transformed society in more ways than one can imagine. When the internet became available to the public in 1990 under the name "World Wide Web," the world had no idea how this new platform of information would change every aspect of society. Even the computer guru Bill Gates had no clue how great the technological transformation would be, signified most obviously by his infamous quote: "640K ought to be enough for anyone." Of course, even a basic webpage today contains more data than 640 kilobytes. From economic to social, the internet has given the people around the world the chance to communicate with each other, overcoming the impasse created by distance that ruled economic and social barriers since the beginning of time. However, even after the internet's introduction, improvements and innovations have made it even more a viable and valuable part of life. With "The Internet of Things" swallowing up more household items every day, the internet has quickly transitioned from a simple social or economic platform into an integral part of society that the world could not properly exist without. One of the greatest improvements within the internet has been the search engine integration which allows users to search the vast library of web pages without more knowledge than the average citizen would possess. Today, the leading internet search engine is Google and the two masterminds behind the search engine giant continue to improve the genius of the web browser. Larry Page and Sergey Brin were just college students when they founded the world's leading search engine but today, their drive for success is hardly over. In Larry's mind, an opportunity to change society and the world is what fuels his constant drive for success. "If you're changing the world," writes Larry, "...you're working on important things. You're excited to get up in the morning." With such excitement becoming the theme of the duo, the success of Google is merely beginning.

Larry's Early Life

While Larry Page would meet his greatest success during his teamwork with Sergey Brin, he would not meet the Russian technologist until his days at Stanford. On March 26, 1973, Larry Page was born to Carl Victor Page, Senior and his wife Gloria, in East Lansing, Michigan. During his childhood, Larry notes that his family followed the strict religious guidelines of the Jewish faith, though Larry did not share this allegiance to Judaism and he is not currently a member or follower of any major religion. Larry's father, Carl, was a vigorous worker who completed his Ph.D. in computer science during Larry's childhood. It was actually Carl who gave Larry his early foundation and love for computer science. Carl proved to be an adept computer technician who was regarded in high esteem by his colleagues in computer science. During an exposé on computer programming, BBC reporter Will Smale gave Carl high praise in referring to him as "the pioneer in computer science and artificial intelligence." Carl worked as a computer programmer at Michigan State University while his wife and mother to Larry, Gloria, also worked as a computer programmer but at Lyman Briggs College, in addition to being a part time employee at Michigan State University. Larry's household resembled what he refers to as the "stereotypical" computer programmer's house, noting that it "was usually a mess,

with computers, science and technology

magazines and *Popular Science* magazines all over the place." During his childhood, Larry's parents instilled in him a desire for reading, as he recalls, "I remember spending a huge amount of time poring over books and magazines." It was during these long periods of reading that Larry became so adept in his worldview of computers. Though a recent innovation and still lacking maturity, the realm of computers was growing almost as quickly as Larry was.

Larry's parents were very encouraging and supportive of his interest in computer innovation. Larry notes that his parents provided anything he needed to grow in his understanding of computers and technology. While Larry's love revolved around computers, he also held great esteem for the fine arts genre, being proficient in both flute and music composition during his childhood. For every year starting in middle school, Larry spend a few weeks of his summer at the Interlochen Arts Camp in Interlochen, Michigan, a prestigious musical camp that was home to numerous child prodigies in the United States. Larry notes that his interest in music fueled his interest in computer science since he was forced to practice his flute patiently as a high schooler. "In music, you're very cognizant of time," notes Larry. "Time is like the primary thing. If you think about it from a music point of view, if you're a percussionist, you hit something, it's got to happen in milliseconds, fractions of a second." Larry's fine understanding of timing allowed him to pursue faster technology and computers. Eventually, this drive for speed would lead to his own internet browser being among the top five fastest internet browsers in the world.

When Larry was six years old, he was given his first glance at a computer and from there, it was love at first sight. Larry notes that with his house being full of technology, he would often "play with the stuff lying around." Most of this "stuff" lying around was actually technology that his parents had discarded with little intent to ever use again, but had unintentionally laid the foundation for the love for computers that would create Google. Larry's future in computers was cemented at a young age when he used a word programming application on his parents' computer to complete an assignment for class. Larry notes that he was the "first kid in my elementary school to turn in an assignment from a word processor." Larry's teachers hardly knew how to react to the technological advancement of their star pupil. Larry had an older brother who showed him the value in disassembling items to see how they actually worked. This would do more than create a hunger for knowledge in Larry; it is what Larry credits with creating the desire for his now company. Larry explains, "from a very early age, I also realized I wanted to invent things. So I became really interested in technology and business. Probably from when I was 12, I knew I was going to start a company eventually." While Larry would have years of education ahead of him before he actually started his own company, the spark had been lit and the fuel of desire would only grow the flame.

Beginning in 1975, Larry would attend the Okemos Montessori School in the small city of Okemos, Michigan. In 1991, he completed his high school education at East Lansing High School, and then beginning in 1991 he would attend the University of Michigan in pursuit of a degree in computer science. However, Larry had not met the person who would transform his life and become his best friend, Sergey Brin.

Sergey's Early Life

Four months after Larry was born, his famous counterpart Sergey Brin would be born to Eugenia and Mikhail Brin in Moscow, which was in the Soviet Union at the time. Sergey's parents were both recent graduates of Moscow State University where they had learned an extensive history in fields of both mathematics and those requiring mathematics. Today, Sergey's father is employed as a teacher of mathematics at the University of Maryland, while his mother is currently a researcher at the Goddard Space Flight Center of NASA. During Sergey's childhood, his family occupied a small, three-room apartment nestled in downtown Moscow. The family would stay in Moscow until 1977 when Sergey's father attended a mathematics conference in Warsaw, Poland. After returning from the conference, Sergey's father became inspired to emigrate from Moscow and set his sights on the freedoms of Poland. Sergey's father began the moving process by applying for an exit visa in the latter portion of 1978 but his plans went amiss when his current work supervisors were informed of his decision to leave. Sergey's father was immediately released from his job and his mother was forced to leave her job as well. With no income and no way to pay for their emigration, Sergey's parents were forced to assumed part-time work until their exit visa was approved. For many months, Sergey's parents would work odd jobs around their neighborhood and in convenience stores, enduring several instances where their exit visas were denied. Due to his family being Jewish, Sergey's father was denied an exit visa for exclusionary reasons. Finally, almost eight months after the initial exit visa was denied, Sergey's family was finally afforded exit visas and allowed to immigrate to Vienna. Sergey's father was highly interested in teaching at the University of Maryland but was unable to secure an immediate position there. For five-year-old Sergey, his recollection of moving is very faint but he remains eternally grateful for his parent's sacrifice, as emigrating led him to Larry Page.

Finally, almost five months after moving from the Soviet Union, Sergey's father was able to finalize a teaching contract with the University of Maryland and the family moved from Vienna to Maryland with the assistance of Anatole Katok and the Hebrew Immigrant Aid Society. During his elementary years, Sergey would attend Paint Branch Montessori School located in Adelphi, Maryland while his father would also homeschool him when he came home from elementary school. With his father being among the highest of qualified math teachers at the University of Maryland, Sergey was given a solid foundation in mathematics while his parents ensured that he also maintained his bilingual status, speaking both English and Russian. For high school, Sergey would attend the Eleanor Roosevelt High School in Greenbelt, Maryland where he graduated in 1990. While Larry was attending the University of Michigan for his undergraduate degree in Computer Science, Sergey would enroll at the Big Ten conference rival, University of Maryland. After three years of college, Sergey graduated with his bachelor's degree in Computer Science while also taking home several prestigious honors for his academic performance. Also astounding, Sergey was a mere 19 years old when he graduated from the University of Maryland. Around the same time, Larry graduated from the University of Michigan and began contemplating pursuing his master's degree. While Larry would eventually decide on Stanford University, he had no idea that his choosing Stanford was more than the choice of a good education; he had also just chosen the college that would put him in contact with his eventual business partner, Sergey Brin.

A New Friendship

In 1993, Sergey began his graduate studies in computer science at Stanford University, still unaware of the existence of Larry Page. Larry had built a name for himself at the University of Michigan, mainly through the introduction of two proposals that he claimed could revolutionize on-campus travel. The first idea included an automated train system on campus that would alleviate congestion while also not using precious funding since it was driverless. The second idea was centered on a plan for a business that would create music through the use of an automated synthesizer, a program that would make new music every time new stipulations were entered into the algorithm. While neither idea would come to fruition, Larry's genius was on full display and it would be these ideas that eventually introduced Larry to Sergey. Shortly after arriving on the Stanford campus, both Larry and Sergey took a break from moving into their rooms to attend an orientation session. It was at this event that the famed duo would first meet. As fate would have it, the two wound up sitting next to each other at the meeting, and they were overjoyed to hear that the other was in the same study at Stanford. While Sergey had been initially interested in simply obtaining a masters degree in computer science, Larry was able to eventually convince him to try his hand at a PhD in computer science. This degree would later be abandoned for his job at Google but for now, his relationship with Larry would begin to blossom into so much more. Ironically, Larry and Sergey did no agree on many subjects during many of their initial conversations but after a while, it became evident that they were growing close in friendship. Eventually, Sergey notes that the two "became intellectual soulmates and close friends." With the budding friendship, it was clear that the two were destined to create something great together.

Within their first discussion, it came to light that Larry was studying "the concept of inferring the importance of a research paper from its citations in other papers" while Sergey was studying data mining. Within their first month of friendship, the two began working on a paper that when completed, would be called "The Anatomy of a Large-Scale Hypertextual Web Search Engine." This would lay the foundation for the eventual search engine, Google, though Sergey and Larry were originally only interested in creating the search engine on a small-scale basis. Previous research had been compiled on the subject and together, Sergey and Larry began working on sifting through the data so that they could compile a functioning search engine. To make the process much easier, Sergey and Larry created the PageRank algorithm, which assigned a rank value to every web page with existing data on a search engine. The result allowed them to see the most pertinent data first but also gave the two more inspiration for creating a search engine that the average user could operate. In its simplest form, the PageRank algorithm analyzed a web page and its content by validating the external links established on the page. Essentially, a web page was deemed more valuable if it had more external citations, a claim that Larry was most interested in with his validation of research papers.

While working on the data for research, Larry was also taxed with his studies as a Ph.D. candidate at Stanford University. Sergey had similar requirements but was not in the Ph.D. program during the same time that Larry was. This time of research was during the same time that Larry was in search of a good theme for his dissertation, which he decided to correlate with his study on the world wide web. Larry chose the topic of mathematical properties within the world wide web and used his studies with Sergey as his foundation. Larry's work supervisor, Terry Winograd, greatly encouraged the topic and Larry credited this reassurance as being the support he needed for his inspiration. Among the other ideas Larry had been deciding between was the science of self-driving cars and telepresence. During this period of history in the world wide web, the presence of backlinks, or external web page links, on a website allowed that web page to be seen more often than other web pages with similar content. When reviewing Larry's work later, author John Battelle wrote, "The entire Web was loosely based on the premise of citation—after all, what is a link but a citation? If he could devise a method to count and qualify each backlink on the web, as Page puts it: 'the web would become a more valuable place.'" With this as his motto, Larry completed "The Anatomy of a Large-Scale Hypertextual Web Search Engine" and published the document online. During the next five years, that document would become the most downloaded document within the topic of science. In an exposé, John Battelle exposed how Larry and Serge were able to unearth such a weighty topic for technological research. "At the time Page conceived BackRub, the web comprised an estimated 10 million documents with an untold number of links between them" writes Battelle. "The computing resources required to crawl such a beast were well beyond the usual bounds of a student project. Unaware of exactly what he was getting into, Page began building out his crawler. The idea's complexity and scale lured Brin to the job. A polymath who had jumped from project to protect without settling on a thesis topic, he found the premise behind BackRub fascinating. 'I talked to lots of research groups around the school,' Brin recalls, 'and this was the most exciting project, both because it tackled the web, which represents human knowledge, and because I liked Larry.'" While the topic would create one of the leading scientific research papers of the day, the true victory from such a research paper was the recognition that the world wide web was a tool but lacked direction, direction that Sergey and Larry could bring.

With the research paper as their guide, Larry and Sergey began operations to create the next greatest search engine. Using Larry's room as the staging ground, the two began creating an internet connection using harvested parts from various computers that had been given to them over the years. With Larry's room being used as the database operation center, the two set up Sergey's room as their office where they programmed the computer programs and tested them. For weeks while the two tested various networking scenarios, the Stanford technical network complained of technical glitches around campus. However, it would be years before the secret of what Sergey and Larry were working on would be revealed. After weeks of programming, the two finally created the prototype of Google and released it to some of their programming friends. Their friends used the new search engine extensively, further causing the Stanford Network to fall apart during busy hours. The initial prototype of Google lacked the aesthetics it contains today due to Sergey and Larry's limited knowledge of network graphics. With the search engine programmed using HTML, the computer language the duo was most familiar with, the page often crashed, leaving Larry and Sergey to constantly monitor the page for maintenance. It should be noted that during this time, the search engine was not referred to as Google but merely acted as a faster search engine with more complete results and was called BackRub. As a sentimental connection toward the website began to give way to those using it for its professional qualities, the increased usage necessitated the use of more servers. Finally, after almost two years of research and programming, the first BackRub search engine was opened to all users. However, the search engine was still only accessible from the Stanford website.

While Sergey and Larry are credited with the origin of Google, there is another person who lacks recognition. Scott Hassan was actually the lead programmer for Google, as Larry and Sergey were involved with more of the hardware structure than the software structure. However, Hassan would leave the team of programmers prior to the initial launch of Google, leaving his name almost completely excluded from Google's legendary story. Today, Hassan works as the founder and operator of Willow Garage, a laboratory dedicated to the study of robots and their usefulness within society.

Growing Pains for Google

In a description of BackRub, the backbone of Google, Larry wrote: "BackRub is written in Java and Python and runs on several Sun Ultras and Intel Pentiums running Linux. The primary database is kept on a Sun Ultra Series II with 28 GB of disk. Scott Hassan and Alan Steremberg have provided a great deal of very talented implementation help. Sergey Brin has also been very involved and deserves many thanks." The greatest tool of BackRub that truly separated it from the competing search engines was its querying tool. In an interview, Larry said, "We realized that we had a querying tool. It gave you a good overall ranking of pages and ordering of follow-up pages." With the ability to rank pages, users found BackRub so much easier to use than the other search engines, and the usage of BackRub began to slowly increase. As Larry and Sergey watched, the daily searches reached 10,000 in one day, to which Larry replied, "Maybe, this is really good." While

BackRub was still in a state of infancy and was immensely immature compared to the search engines of today, the technological media of the day began to recognize the power that a functioning search engine brought. In an article titled "Google the Gutenberg," the author compares the effectiveness of BackRub (the predecessor to Google) to the influence that the Gutenberg printing press created with its introduction of the Bible to Europe. "In 1440" the article explains, "Johannes Gutenberg introduced Europe to the mechanical printing press, printing Bibles for mass consumption. The technology allowed for books and manuscripts—originally replicated by hand—to be printed at a much faster rate, thus spreading knowledge and helping to usher in the European Renaissance. Google [originally called BackRub] has done a similar job." With BackRub on the internet and accessible by all, Sergey and Larry set their sights on something that had never been done before: the digitizing of books and other items for reading on the internet.

In 1998, Sergey and Larry went to their families for funding in hopes of renting a small garage large enough to house their servers and programming computers. After searching around for the lowest deal, Sergey and Larry found the garage that would become among the most famous garages: a small location in Menlo Park, California. Within a few weeks, the duo had their servers up and running and BackRub was online once again. During this time, Larry and Sergey prophesized that their search engine would become superior to the other search engines through one basic element: popularity. While many of the current search engines would provide results based on how many times the search term appeared on the page, Sergey and Larry proposed that the better search results would be those that were connected to other links around the web. Prior to its incorporation, Sergey, Larry, Reajeev Motwani, and Terry Winograd published a paper describing what they were now referring to as Google. The search engine was supposed to be the greatest the world had ever seen and its early testers devoted their support to the truth of this statement. Two other contributors that were greatly influential in creating Google were Hector Garcia-Molina and Jeff Ullman.

After releasing the Google search engine, Sergey and Larry watched as the users of Google increased daily. Convinced that the search engine was destined to become something far greater, Andy Bechtolsheim, the famous co-founder of Sun Microsystems, donated $100,000 through a check addressed to Google, Inc. This provided a small problem: Google had not yet been incorporated. Sergey and Larry were waiting to see the initial success of Google before they paid the fees associated with incorporating the company. For two weeks, the check would lay dormant in Sergey's personal safe, before the two finally became convinced that incorporating the company was the next great step towards the promotion of Google.

With finances tight during its inception, Google was eager for donations from angel investors. Two other major donors in addition to Bechtolsheim were Jeff Bezos of Amazon and Ram Shiram, a millionaire investor. David Cheriton from Stanford University would also be among the first to contribute financially to Google.

The first domain name for Google was actually "Googol," a derivation of the number representing a number equivalent to a number with 100 mathematical zeros. This name was chosen because Larry asserted that the search engine would search nearly that many databases before returning the results to the server. With Google finally incorporated, the leadership team for Google began to assemble. Larry was named CEO while Sergey would be named the co-founder and act as President of the company. It should be noted that despite being named the co-founder, Sergey was merely an aid to the creation of Google, not even the one who originated the idea. While Sergey would act as Larry's closest friend while being an invaluable asset to the organization, some members of the press have been quick to dispel the shared responsibility of Google between Larry and Sergey. Nicholas Carlson wrote: "While Google is often thought of as the invention of two young computer whizzes, Sergey and Larry, Larry and Sergey, the truth is that Google is a creation of Larry Page, helped along by Sergey Brin." While Larry is quick to call Sergey his co-founder and share an equal share of the glory of Google with him, many within the technical world have asserted that Google is largely the brainchild of Larry Page.

In 1999, Larry began testing a variety of sequences involving different sizes of servers, attempting to create as much room for maximum data. Google had grown so quickly that Larry and Sergey had been forced to move the servers out of the garage in Menlo Park and into a variety of warehouses around the area. With the multitude of servers, Google began beating its opponents by more than double their download speed. This of course led to more traffic, which led to more financial input and more growth for Google. Google's growth was skyrocketing, and by 2000 the company had surpassed one billion uniform resource locaters (URLs). With such a vast library, Google was able to call itself the most authoritative search engine and its usage only increased. In a news release on June 26 of the same year, NEC Research Institute wrote, "There are more than one billion web pages online today and Google is providing access to 560 million full-text indexed web pages and 500 million partially indexed URLs." It was coming to the day when if a company wanted maximum exposure on the world wide web, they turned to Google and made sure that their website was easily accessible from Google's homepage.

In 1999, many working for Google were wondering about the state of the finances. Though the company was growing rapidly, there were still concerns about the debt within the organization and whether or not it could survive the coming changes to the internet. Sergey and Larry settled all fears with a $25 million round of investing that included the major financial contributions of Kleiner Perkins and Sequoia Capital. For those worrying about the financial future of Google, those fears would be dispelled soon. Google was only a short distance away from its greatest expansion yet.

The Early Authority of Google, Inc.

In 1999, Google's home office was moved to Palo Alto, California where it was left to incubate among the many other technical startups in the area. Heeding their own disdain for search engines that were cluttered with advertisements, Sergey and Larry vowed to never allow their search engine to be completely funded by advertisements. Google's initial advertisements involved search word inquiry, which essentially meant that Google would supply advertisements based on the search term requested. Such a move contradicted the duo's earlier stance on no advertisement and many wondered if the proposition of millions of dollars had distracted them from true success. Google received its biggest promotion yet in 2000 when YAHOO! announced that Google would serve as the primary search engine for their website. This transition shocked the leading search engine of the time, Inktomi, and made many think that Google was only years away from becoming just as powerful, if not more so, than Inktomi. While the growth Google was experiencing was benefiting their finances mightily, it soon became evident that there were serious leadership flaws within the company. Soon, Google would weather its biggest storm yet as its CEO would divide some of the unity.

In 2001, Larry became controlling of the company's projects, so controlling in fact that he demanded to be in charge of everything the company was producing. While Larry attempted to fire every project manager, he would fall short and eventually become the subject of great disdain from his fellow employees and subordinates. Larry's entire premise for firing all of the project managers came from an inherent desire to control every aspect of business while also exhibiting a lack of trust towards everyone in the company. Larry also noted that he was wary of people supervising projects when they themselves had equal or even less authority on the subject. With these tenants fresh in his mind, Larry formulated what he would call his five rules of business, which are as follows: First, "Don't delegate. Do everything you can yourself to make things go faster." In Larry's mind, the time it took to explain projects among those involved was a waste. Larry would rather control every project since he would not have to explain the project management objectives to anyone else. Second, "Don't get in the way if you're not adding value. Let the people actually doing the work talk to each other while you go do something else." In Larry's mindset, the value of contribution was only as powerful and valued as the information that was pertinent to the project. According to Larry, these projects did not need any more people to merely "support" the projects or do the dirty work for the project. Third, "Don't be a bureaucrat." Larry asserted that the best kinds of leaders were those who involved themselves with their subordinates and participated in the projects they were overseeing. Larry equated being a bureaucrat with being a dictator. Fourth, "Ideas are more important than age. Just because someone is a junior doesn't mean they don't deserve respect and cooperation." This rule held personal influence due to Larry's past with bullying in school. A skinny child, Larry had often been the subject of bullying and had often seen his ideas trampled on as a byproduct of his being bullied. Finally, "The worst thing you can do is stop someone from doing something by saying, 'No. Period.' If you say no, you have to help them find a better way to get it done." While these ideas were mainly rooted in Larry's disdain for empowerment, he maintains that these ideas allowed Google to establish a sturdier foundation amidst the troubles of a young company.

Larry's model of leadership ultimately failed within the company and resulted in a large contingent of employees who were highly angered at his lack of empowerment. Though

Larry claimed to be against dictators, many of Larry's subordinates felt that he did not respect their opinions and did not foster an environment conducive to growth. However, there was one element of Larry's leadership that was eventually accepted and continues to be accepted to this day. Larry's assertion that those with fewer qualifications than those they are overseeing have no business overseeing such people or projects. Even today, numerous technical companies in Silicon Valley use this leadership principle. Among the aspects most stressed by Larry was the subject of time. Larry believed that the greatest factor of differentiation from other search engines was that of delay and time. Should Google grow slower as some of its predecessors had, Larry feared that the large contingent of followers would be tempted to join another search engine, abandoning Google. When new projects were presented to Larry, his first question always centered on whether or not the proposal would improve the time between the initiation and completion of the search results. As part of this initiative, Larry was also very concerned with the appearance of the Google homepage and demanded that the page be uncluttered. Larry's leadership took a major blow when it was suggested that he remove himself as CEO of Google so that the company could further develop its global initiative. Among those supporting the idea most fiercely was Kleiner Perkins Caufield and Byers, a large venture capital firm that threatened to remove their financial support of the company unless Larry stepped aside as CEO. According to Kleiner Perkins Caufield & Byers, Larry was not capable of nor built to "create a world-class management team." Though completely opposed to the idea at first, Larry finally conceded and agreed that the idea would lead to greater financial and business growth for Google. Among those most influential in persuading him to step aside as CEO were other CEOs Steve Jobs of Apple and Andrew Grove of Intel. The chairman of Novel, Eric Schmidt, removed himself from his position to assume the same position within Google and Larry was finally persuaded to retire as CEO of Google so that he could take on his new position as President of Products. Though the early days of Google were fraught with a power struggle, Larry Page gave Google a secure foundation for success.

In 2002, the leadership of Google was given a serious boost of esteem when Sergey Brin was announced as being one of the top 100 innovators in the world who were under 35 years old. Larry was also a part of this list, as was Steve Jobs. The following year, the major growth to Google had warranted the prospects of yet another move. Google was currently leasing two locations where they housed servers and other computers. The leadership of Google finally found another building in Mountain View, California. This would become almost as famous as the garage in Menlo Park, although the garage would and continues to draw more tourists every year. Within a few years, the offices at the Mountain View complex would become known as the Googleplex, which was a derivation from the word googolplex, which had of course been the company's first domain name. Google would only lease the property for three years before eventually purchasing the land from SGI for a phenomenal deal of $319 million.

At this point in the history of Google, the company was watching the word "Google" transform from merely the name of search engine to becoming an actual word. Many Millennials were already familiar with the phrase "Google It!" which led to the word Google being added to the dictionary. In the Oxford English Dictionary, the word means, "to use the Google search engine to obtain information on the internet." Within the same year, Eric Schmidt would be given the title of CEO in addition to his current position as Chairman of the Board of Directors. With Google growing and becoming ever more laden with the financial prowess of advertising, many thought Google to be in a financial position that no other search engine was enjoying. However, Google was about to embark on another journey that would lead to its finances exploding through the boundaries of what anyone had every imagined for the company.

The IPO of Google

In 2004, Larry and Sergey flirted with the idea of launching initial public offering (IPO) for Google, an act that would make Google's finances shared but also open the door to an untapped stream of revenue. Larry and Sergey had been recently introduced on ABC World News Tonight as the Persons of the Week, further vaulting them and Google into greater fame. With the talks of an IPO growing stronger every day, Sergey, Larry, and the CEO Eric sought to create job security within their own positions by signing agreements to work for Google until at least 2024, exactly twenty years from when the agreement was signed. With such an agreement in place, Larry and Sergey convinced the board of directors that they were indeed ready for their IPO. After the IPO had been introduced, Google announced that it would be offering almost 19,700,000 shares for a price per share of $85. Under a special computer program that Google contracted Morgan Stanley and Credit Suisse to create, the shares were sold online using an auction format. At the completion of the sale, Google had raised over $1.67 billion in capital and had increased their market capitalization to over $23 billion. Google, a mere search engine that simply brought people closer to websites, had successful raised enough capital to grow their company over tenfold in the coming years. Throughout the initial public offering, Schmidt always asked Sergey and Larry what their voice would be on every matter. Larry was even the one who signed the initial public offering. Despite the recent power shift from Larry to Schmidt, Schmidt consistently included the co-founders on plans and projects. At the completion of the first year, it was found that Larry was worth an estimated billion dollars. With Larry only being 30 years old at the time, he truly demonstrated his genius in both business and computer science to the world.

    In the latter portion of 2005, Google's financial strength was shown to the public when it was announced that the company had produced almost 700% in growth. The astounding increase was due in large part to the digitizing of society. Internet marketing was quickly overtaking the other marketing strategies as the most popular and most highly grossing method of getting the message of one's company to the eye of the public. The Washington Post completed a story that included the dramatic increase in profit for Google and the increase in investors that came primarily from the free publicity Google was beginning to receive. With newspapers, television, and magazines experiencing lower usage number due to the networking of America, the internet was beginning to overtake society while showing its growing influence.

In 2006, Schmidt further endeared himself to Sergey and Larry when he set out to establish an executive team for Google. Despite being trusted with the leadership of the company, Schmidt was certain to allow Sergey and Brin the final say on whether or not a person was to be a part of the executive team for Google. This move created more trust between the co-founders and Larry and led to the relationship largely becoming symbiotic. This trust would be crucial when Schmidt later went on to create his own sales force management system, which Larry and Sergey readily accepted. Though the leadership had changed within Google, those at Google still regard Larry as the supreme authority over the business.

While Google was growing rapidly, the board of directors suggested making Google more influential across the value chain, meaning that Google would control some of the companies it was currently servicing. One of these companies was a growing technical startup named Android. Considered to be a small-time technical company that lacked direction, Larry and Sergey saw this as an opportunity to grow Google and possibly invest in the future of both Google and technology. For $50 million, Android was acquired by Google and Larry immediately set out to position the company as one that would "place handheld computers in the possession of consumers so that they could access Google anywhere." This statement would cause investors to question how much of the power as CEO Larry had truly given up, given that Larry purchased Android for half of a billion dollars without the permission of Schmidt. However, Schmidt handled the usurping of his authority graciously and did not bring up the matter with the board of directors.

After Android had been purchased by Google, Larry devoted much of his attention to the phone software and became dedicated to providing the best phone with the best search engine to the public. For the next three years, Larry and the CEO of Android, Andy Rubin spent almost every workday together, perfecting the operating system they believed could transform the technology of America. This investment of time would pay off in 2008 when the company introduced the G-1 from T-Mobile. The G-1, while developed by a different company, became the first phone to operate under the Android platform and largely pushed the platform to the success and fame it enjoys today. Android would continue to grow and in 2010, it was revealed that the company had overtaken Apple as the leader of handset sales with a market share of 17.2%. Though most of the success of Android is attributed to the Android board of directors, the financial input from Android has benefited Google nicely and has more than paid for the initial investment of $50 million that Larry made so many years earlier. A few months after overtaking Apple as the world's leading handset operating system, Android became the most popular platform within cell phone operating systems. For Larry, the success of Android boosted his self esteem from the low it had experienced following his removal as CEO. Larry had his confidence back and Google was going to be the greatest heir of this confidence and success.

In 2006, Larry and Sergey decided to add to the impressive list of Google acquisitions and invest in another company that would place them in more control of their overall value chain. With file sharing being the latest rage on the internet, small websites such as YouTube were popping up but all lacked the major funding necessary to support their growth. Out of all the file sharing websites, Larry saw the most potential in YouTube, considering it already housed videos from well-known athletes. After one month of negotiating, the two parties reached a deal and Google purchased YouTube for over $1.5 billion in Google stock. The price was considered well beyond what YouTube was truly worth but both Schmidt and Larry agreed that the company would provide enough advertising to make the necessary return. While Google was still transforming the leadership of YouTube, the board of directors approved another acquisition. This time, it was a company that would become among the most fruitful for Google. DoubleClick was an established online ad agency that had cornered the market on digital advertising within Google. After extensive negotiating, Google and DoubleClick agreed to the price tag of $3.1 billion and Google took over the leadership of the company. Tracing an exact correlation, DoubleClick would be Google's most fruitful acquisition, now under the name of Google Ad Services. What was once a company that took advantage of the need for a faster search engine was now a company that was firmly atop the pedestal as the greatest search engine in the world. True to his original stipulations for Google, Larry had also ensured that Google was the fastest internet search engine and the coming years would spell much of the same success Google was currently enjoying.

Continued Growth and a New CEO

While Google was flourishing as a technical company, Larry and Sergey began investing in some social responsibility with their added resources. One of the largest social causes that the duo invested in was the offshore wind power development that directly aids the East Coast Power Grid. Google has promised to provide all of the necessary funding to build and power one of the power plans, with eleven more needing to be built to fully power the East Coast. In addition to investing in social responsibility, Larry and Sergey registered the domain name www.google.org as a domain that is completely centered on providing awareness of social disasters or areas for the public to contribute to health and natural disasters. While the majority of Google's social responsibility comes through their philanthropic efforts, they also note that several of their projects are directly designed to aid the public. One of those public aids is a self-driving car that Sergey has essentially taken control of. The car is driven using "artificial intelligence" and is powered by a robotic sensor that runs off of the various cameras mounted to the sides of the car. Without the necessary safety requirements to protect a driver, these cars would be manufactured much lighter and would also allow for less emission since the self-driving cars would be more efficient. With Sergey being an investor in Tesla Motors, there is hope that the car company will one day allow Google to provide some of the technical support they have acquired in their own driverless cars. Tesla Motors has produced several driverless cars but lacks the software needed to convert the self-driving cars to a grid. In time, Google hopes to provide this service to Tesla, paving the way for a completely driverless world.

    Out of the two co-founders, Sergey has proven himself to be the more financially savvy one, being an investor in several Fortune 500 companies. Another one of Sergey's spotlight investments is in Space Adventures, a space travel organization owned and operated by Eric Anderson. While Sergey provided the large investment to further the necessary science required to send people to space for travel purposes, Sergey also guaranteed himself a flight aboard one of the space travel flights when space travel becomes more common. In 2007, Sergey's personal life was given national recognition when it was revealed that had gotten marred to Anne Wojcicki who was a biotech analyst in addition to trading stock. After almost one year of marriage, the couple would welcome their first child to the world, a son, before having another daughter two years later. Though their marriage appeared to be happy, it was revealed that the couple had formally separated in 2013 due to allegations from his wife that Sergey had committed an extramarital affair with the mass marketing director of Project Glass, Google's virtual reality glasses. The separation would last for two years until the two would be formally divorced in

2015. Sergey has long held strong family ties and holds a special bond with his mother as she battles Parkinson's Disease. In 2008, Sergey and his wife established The Brin Wijcicki Foundation which the couple still operates jointly despite their divorce. Additionally, Sergey continues to donate generously to the University of Maryland School of Medicine, which is currently the residence of his mother's treatment. Sergey is a member of the Michael J. Fox Foundation and is a yearly donor of the Hebrew Immigrant Aid Society, the group that aided his father in escaping Moscow so many years earlier. Sergey is a proclaimed Democrat and was a staunch supporter of the campaign for Barak Obama in 2012, donating almost $30,000 to his campaign.

In 2011, Larry had grown enough under the tutelage of Eric Schmidt that the board of directors thought him eligible for the position of CEO again. The timing proved to be perfect as Schmidt was seeking to trade his position as CEO for a less stressful job on the board of directors. Larry jumped at the opportunity to return to his old job and assumed the position of CEO of Google again on April 4, 2011. While Larry had learned a lot under the leadership of Schmidt, the industrial age had greatly grown and the value of Google had also grown. Now, Google was a company with a $180 billion market capitalization along with a task force of over 24,000 people. The Google Larry had stepped down from years ago was long gone—his influence on the world had the potential to be so much greater now. While there was joy around Google the day that Larry assumed his position as CEO, there was also a sense of relief that the man intended for the job had finally graduated from training and was able to take the position with maturity. Shortly before releasing his leadership within the company, Schmidt jokingly told the press that he was removing the adult supervision and that Larry was more than capable to control of the company. For the next few years, Google would attempt to recover what many had referred to as the "lost decade" in which Larry sat in humiliation and watched his leadership position be filled by someone else. However, the honeymoon ended quickly for Larry and soon, there were numerous complaints that he was once again drawing more exclusively into his leadership team and was not visible to the employees anymore. For those within Google, this seemed all too familiar and many feared that Larry would soon be stepping down again. However, after a short while, Larry began walking through his employees' offices more often and introduced what he had been working on, a large policy on bullying that he claimed was needing amidst the changing work environment. Contradictory to his first stint as CEO, Larry began experimenting with autonomy among his employees, a gamble that largely paid off. Larry asserted that the employees taxed with oversight of the divisions he warranted "irreplaceable" to the company should be given more authority and trust. Backing this claim, Larry created the "L Team," essentially an executive leadership team that worked with Larry on a daily basis while relaying his expectations to the employees. Perhaps the most significant move immediately following his ascension to CEO was the placement of a CEO within all of the Google annexes. These would include the businesses of YouTube, AdWords, and Google Search. Whereas once Larry had detested additional leadership that contradicted his own, he now welcomed the leadership as teamwork and supported the presentation of ideas that opposed his. In addition to supporting new leadership, Larry further expounded on his anti-bullying policy that included verbal fighting within the organization. For those not yet convinced that Larry's administrative policy had changed, this should have served as proof enough, considering Larry was known for being especially combative during his first tenure as CEO. In comparing the first and second tenures of CEO under Larry, the greatest transformation was the expansion of teamwork within his team. Among the further differences that spread from the transformation was the consolidation of all of Google's products. With all of the products under one department, Larry hired the help of more designers and the aesthetic transformation of Google's products swept through the media. For Larry, the second time proved to be the difference between being a leader and being a great leader.

For Google, the peak had yet to be reached as the company continued to grow in seemingly every aspect. The company announced tremendous numbers in 2011, with over three billion search requests every day. With such a high workload, the servers at the Google headquarters were taxed and in need of updating. To compensate for this, Google established eleven data centers around the world that each housed over one thousand servers respectfully, each designed to handle the growing workload. With the data requested only growing, it made perfect sense to plan that far into the future. Shortly after upgrading all of their servers, Google announced that they had acquired Motorola Mobility for $12.5 billion, crushing the previous record they had set for Google with the acquisition of DoubleClick. While the other acquisitions had been designed to allow Google to cover more of the value chain in their pursuit of customers, the acquisition of Motorola was largely due to a few ongoing disputes with companies over patent issues. Additionally, Motorola had an additional portfolio of patents that Google thought necessary to their continued growth as both a search engine provider and technological provider. Google was currently in the process of making their own phone and several lawsuits were in the midst of being fought between Google and Apple. With Apple's precious market share of mobile phones being threatened by Google, Apple was not going to let another element of its company be superseded by Google as they had been when Google overtook them through Android as the world's most popular mobile device platform. With

Motorola now a part of Google, Larry and Sergey were able to concentrate on growing their customer base with the eventual release of a mobile phone.

In early 2013, Larry, as part of his transformation within leadership initiative, discontinued almost seventy of Google's products so that the resources could be efficiently pooled among the few remaining products. Additionally, Larry appointed a chief of design to Google so that all of the new products would be released under the same platform and appearance. Jon Wiley from the Google Search design team nicknamed the new Google product transformation as "Project Kennedy" since Larry had once referred to the feasibility of his dreams for Google as "moonshots." As the technical world watched with bated breath, Google attempted to once again unify their product appearance. Previously, Google had launched an initiative called "Kanna" which was aimed at redesigning all of the products under one similar look.

However, the project failed miserably due to the large variety in products that was represented. Larry was hopeful that with the smaller group, the transformation would actually be successful this time. For the next few weeks following the release of the plans for "Project Kennedy," Larry constantly traveled to New York City where he would meet with the lead designers for Google and work together to form a "cohesive vision" for the future of Google products. Between June of 2011 and January of 2013, Google released several products as part of the "Project Kennedy" transformation. One of the first reviews of the products noted that they were centered on "refinement, white space, cleanliness, elasticity, usefulness, and most of all simplicity." While the products' appearance had changed greatly, they had not deviated from Larry's consistent stipulation of faster speed. With the exterior completely transformed, Larry and Serge set out to transform the interface of the software, a project that Larry described as "designing and developing a true

UI framework that transforms Google's application software into a beautiful, mature, accessible, and consistent platform for all of its users." Ironically, the project team tasked with transforming the software of Google to meet the requirements of Larry and Sergey was extremely small and would never be introduced to the public.

Called the greatest transformation of Google, the time period of Google from 2011-2014 very well might have been the Golden Age of Google. However, only time will tell when the greatest days of success for Google were and for now, the numbers for Google only continue to rise.

Google in 2012 and Beyond

In 2012, Google announced that it had surpassed its previous mark of $38 billion and had generated over $50 billion in revenue. The previous yield of $38 billion had been set only one year previous, meaning that Google had generated an increase of over $12 billion in only one year. At a board of directors meeting, Larry announced: "We ended 2012 with a strong quarter. Revenues were up 36% year-on-year and 8% quarter-on-quarter. And we hit $50 billion in revenue for the first time last year—not a bad achievement in just a decade and a half." With investors extremely pleased with the direction Google was taking financially, Larry and Sergey felt confident in any acquisition that would give them either more market share in a market they currently held a share of or a market they could control from a point in their value chain. During an interview in which Larry revealed the criteria he held for acquisitions, Larry noted that he always asked himself if he valued the acquisition as one values a toothbrush. Explaining his criteria, Larry stated: "Is it something you will use once or twice a day, and does it make your life better?" Using such a criteria, Google has only dominated through its acquisitions and has yet to acquire a business that has not worked well with the Google marketing.

In 2011, Larry and Sergey entered a new market with Google; however, this market would be one they would enter as both second movers and without the aid of an acquisition. To date, Google had not done anything more than advertise within the social media industry. However, Larry and Sergey both felt that a large portion of Google's target audience was in this group and was being unreached by Google. In a rush of programming and design, Larry and Sergey designed a social media website they called Google+. In essence, it was supposed to imitate friends hanging out, with the videoconferencing and messaging functions all resembling terminology from friends hanging out together. After only three days of testing through mainly employees, Google+ was released to the public The initial reaction was not as excited as Larry or Sergey thought or hoped it would be but the website did serve as a distraction from Facebook, which was rumored to be entering the mobile phone platform.

Despite the poor numbers presented in Google+, which turned out to be Google's worst promotion yet, Sergey and Larry still felt it necessary to acquire any businesses that had the potential to add value to their company. The next company that would become Google's project was Waze, a popular crowd-sharing app within the locations industry. The app would add tremendous value to the company since Google was not yet actively involved in the location industry beyond Google Maps, which had seen increased competition from Apple Maps. When the acquisition was completed, Waze was purchased for $966 million and almost immediately fell under several lawsuits, some from the government that alleged that the app's notification of nearby police officers violates federal law. Many of these lawsuits are still being fought in court to this day. To isolate Google from the impending lawsuits, Google has opted to retain Waze as an independent entity that simply shares its abilities with Google Maps.

In 2012, it was revealed that Larry and Sergey co-own a Boeing 767-200 along with the Dornier Alpha Jet. One element of this ownership that has come under tremendous scrutiny is the price tag of $1.3 million that is paid each year simply to house the large jets. Many accuse Larry and Sergey of violating their own standard on renewably energies with two planes that create more emissions than cars. However, Sergey and Larry maintain that the jets are necessary to the business operations of Google and are used at a minimum.

During the latter portion of 2012, Sergey separated from the day-to-day operations of Google for a brief period while he took a leadership position within the Project Glass program. This project is sponsored by Google and is centered on the research of creating a pair of glasses that can also function as a pair of regular sunglasses or even prescription glasses. The official branch of science associated with this is known as augmented reality head-mounted display, or HMD. While the project would not be completed before Sergey returned to day-to-day operations within Google, the project appears to be closer to the creation of full-line production as Google and Apple race to be the first to release a functional pair of augmented reality glasses.

In 2012, Larry and Sergey orchestrated yet another dramatic product reveal as the newly finished Chromebook was released in May of the same year. The Chromebook marked the first laptop computer that Google had produced along with the first software operating system for a laptop. The software, Chrome OS, was riddled with bugs during its initial release but would eventually be updated to remove the bugs. The Chromebook was marketed as an internet computer that had the ability to store small documents on its drive. Mainly marketed to college students, the Chromebook saw tremendous success during its first release and sold enough to warrant an update to the aesthetics one year later. The same year, Google announced that it would launch a new company named Calico that was actually led by Arthur Levinson of Apple computers. The company was focused on the research of diseases and cures associated with those diseases. The company also sought to show the public that while competition existed between the "Big Four Tech Companies," subjects such as social justice and social responsibility were shared among the core standards of the four companies and also were the responsibility of the four companies as a team. While the group has yet to produce a drug, it remains dedicated to finding cures for and eradicating what were once thought to be incurable diseases.

One year later, Google would acquire DeepMind Technologies from London-based Lila Ibrahim. The company is nestled within the artificial intelligence industry and is a great complement to the augmented reality glasses that Google continues to research. While the financial dealings of the acquisition would never be revealed, it is rumored that the company was acquired for around $400 million. With such an acquisition, Google is considered to be the most robotically advanced company of the Big Four Tech Companies. However, while they continue to be the most advanced in the research of robots and artificial intelligence, Google's revenues continue to come in second behind Apple. For the past four years, Google's valuation in regards to brand recognition is consistently behind Apple, despite Google's Android being more popular on mobile devices than Apple's iOS operating system. To better consolidate the numerous branches of Google and possibly address the problem of brand recognition, Google announced in 2015 that it would be constructing a conglomerate called Alphabet, which would control the various companies of Google. As the leading producer of revenue, Google is regarded as the largest subsidiary under Alphabet but companies such as Google AdSense and Google Glass continues to derive their fair share of attention from the press. With Google controlling the market share on internet servers and search engines, Google and Alphabet agreed to allow Google to operate as the umbrella company for any internet needs Alphabet may have. When the restructuring of Google as a subsidiary of Alphabet was completed, Larry Page shocked Google by announcing that he would be stepping down as CEO of Google so that he could operate as CEO of Alphabet. For Larry, the continued success of Google lay in the hands of the person occupying the seat as CEO of Alphabet and he trusted no one more than himself. Though in a new position, Larry would continue to drive the success of Alphabet just as he had with Google.

A New Era for Google

At a board meeting in the latter portion of 2016, Larry revealed to the board of directors for Alphabet that Google was currently operating in over 40 countries through the direction of 70 offices. As for the engine that powered Google, google.com was listed as the most visited website in the world, dominating its way to the top of a list that it has and continues to dominate. Within the top 100 most visited websites are the Alphabet subsidiaries YouTube and Blogger. The expansion of influence and finances has been accompanied by new issues and new problems. In 2017, Google was host to a myriad of problems when employee James Damore sent a memo throughout the organization that alleged that sexual and racial discrimination existed within the work environment. Damore had been inspired to write the memo after attending a Google diversity program that encouraged the written submission of policies that encourage racism. Angered by an undisclosed matter, James proceeded to pen the letter to Google employees as he was on a flight to China. Referring to the work environment within Google as being "an ideological echo chamber," Damore alleged that the company attempted to correct previous discrimination allegations through reverse discrimination. The meme was initially spread throughout an internal email list before Gizmodo found a copy and published the memo to the internet. Google came under serious scrutiny for the allegations in the memo and many called for a boycott of Google. However, Google responded to the matter by promptly firing Damore on August 7, 2017 and held a press conference in which they asserted: "Part of building an open, inclusive environment means fostering a culture in which those with alternative views, including different political views, feel safe sharing their opinions. But that discourse needs to work alongside the principles of equal employment found in our Code of Conduct policies, and antidiscrimination laws." Sundar Pichai, the CEO who was appointed to his position following the stepping down of Larry, expressed complete faith in the Google Code of Conduct while denying that any reverse discrimination took place. Immediately following his firing, Damore filed a complaint with the National Labor Relations Board, alleging that he had been fired without cause. Before the case made its way to court, Damore would withdraw the claim upon the suggestion of his lawyer who found the firing to be in order. For a few weeks following the incident, various advertisements were posted online calling for a boycott of Google but were subsequently removed when little response was given. Despite the consensus that Google had committed no wrong, several politicians found Pichai's response to the matter concerning and called for his resignation, calls which he continues to ignore.

In late 2018, another incident tested the supremacy of Google. The New York Times published an article titled "How Google

Protected Andy Rubin, the Father of Android" in which they exposed a large number of sexual misconduct allegations within the company's leadership. Immediately following the publication, Google retaliated by referencing the 48 employees they had fired in the last two years for offenses against their policy on sexual misconduct. However, the employees of Google continued to allege that far more than 48 incidents had taken place over the last two years and a global walk out gathered over 20,000 participants on November 1, 2018. Thus far, Google has not made any drastic changes to their sexual misconduct policy while also continuing to maintain that they have handled every serious incident with professionalism.

In early March of 2019, Google added to its list of penetrated industries with the addition of the video game industry. Google launched Google Stadiu, which resembled the online gaming platform Steam and allows users the ability to rent or buy video games to play on their computers. The biggest claim from Google

Stadia is the alleged ability to broadcast the games in 4K resolution, which would trump the performance of Stadia's greatest competitor, Steam. Additionally, the program allows users the ability to upload live content to their YouTube channel since both apps will be integrated into the Google Chrome web browser. The system is still in beta testing and is projected to be released in late 2019.

Legal Issues for Google

In 2019, a deluge of companies facing anti-trust violations from the Department of Justice greatly weakened the trust the American people had in companies and doing transactions online. Specifically, the Department of Justice targeted companies that were harvesting user data without permission before sequentially selling that data to third party companies, once again without the consent of the user. A topic that has become the crux of proposed internet reform for many of the candidates in the 2020 Presidential Election, Google joined the companies accused of such actions on June 3, 2019. Ironically, Larry had previously spoken of the growing anti-trust laws back in 2013 when he noted: "I do not think the internet's under much greater attack than it has been in the past. Governments are now afraid of the internet because of the Middle East stuff, and so they're a little more willing to listen to what I see as a lot of commercial interests that just want to make money by restricting people's freedoms. But they've also seen a tremendous user reaction, like the backlash against SOPA [Stop Online Piracy Act]. I think that governments fight users' freedom at their own peril." While the investigation is ongoing, this is not the first time that Google has been investigated by the Department of Justice for alleged misconduct or privacy violations. In March of 2019, Google paid almost $1.7 billion in fines to the European government for violation of antitrust laws. Even before this, Google was fined twice before by the European Union for violating privacy laws, the combination of the three penalties reaching almost $9 billion.

At the crux of the anti-trust law violation in the European Union is the allegation that Google withheld certain advertisements from companies that had competitors that Google previously held contracts with. Margarethe Vestager, a competition commissioner from the European Union notes: "There was no reason for Google to include these restrictive clauses in its contracts except to keep rivals out of the market." Additionally, the European Union alleges that Google has discriminated within some of the search results for local job listings. Google has issued multiple statements maintaining their innocence in these allegations, noting that while they have had to pay over $9 billion in fees, they have avoided many more fees from the European Union.

Google's legal affairs have cost the company some of its social esteem, denoted no better than by the drop in Fortune magazine's ranking of the best companies to work for. In 2007 and 2008, Google was listed as first on the prestigious list but fell to fourth in 2009 and 2019. This drop is largely associated with the growing concerns about the work environment within Google. However, while receiving a demotion in 2010, Google was also named the most attractive location for college graduates. This ranking is largely due to Google's new initiative to encourage recent graduates to earn their income fairly, noting their three core principles for new employees: "You can make money without doing evil. You can be serious without a suit. Work should be challenging and the challenge should be fun." While the majority of Google's workforce is white men, the National Labor Board has noted no disparity in the proportion of men to women or white to Asian in the company.

The Current Social Responsibility of Google

In 2010, Sergey and Larry established a project that they continue to this day, the Google Fiber project. Under this project, Google is committed to establishing an ultra-high-speed broadband network throughout various American cities, bringing the speedy internet to anywhere from between 50,000 to 500,000 customers. Google Fiber was slightly delayed in its maturity when the conglomeration of Alphabet began. However, the project was moved to completion stage in 2016 and the first customers received their ultra-high-speed internet. At the close of the 2016 year, Google Fiber held over 65,000 customers for its television services while holding an additional 450,000 customers for broadband internet. The service is currently offered in four cities with no intentions to move beyond these cities as

Google has diverted research funding from Google Fiber to its product line.

A similar project would be offered in 2015 when Google announced the proposal for Project Fi, hybrid of Wi-Fi and mobile communications that would bring the two together for more consistent data speeds and lower prices. The project would eventually be renamed Google Fi and would be opened for public use on March 7, 2016. The service would be limited to devices running Android from the time of its inception until November 28, 2018, when the program began supporting iPhones. Google Fi is largely popular due to its ability to connect to virtually any WiFi hotspot through VPNs previously set up through Google. Google Fi continues to grow slowly, though its growth is largely hindered by the $10 price tag that accompanies every gigabyte of additional data.

Larry and Sergey took the social responsibility of Google from the borders of America and announced the beginning of a new initiative called the Google Station in India beginning in September of 2016. The project is mainly focused on providing public WiFi at every train station in India. After only two months of operation, the project had amassed 15,000 users and was available at almost 100 train stations. To date, almost 3.5 million people use the free WiFi every month, spurring Google to promise expanded WiFi at more locations than simply train stations.

While Google may have been started by two guys in a rented garage, it now exists as a company housing almost 100,000 employees who are dedicated to the excellence and speed Google has been providing for years now. Whereas the initial social responsibility of Google was founded in the personal standards of Sergey Brian and Larry Page, the social responsibility is now the heartbeat of the ethics for Google and will continue to lead Google as a reformer of the world in the years to come.

References

Battelle, John. "The Birth of Google." *Wired*, Conde Nast, 26 July 2018, www.wired.com/ 2005/08/battelle/.

"The History of Google." *Internet History Podcast*, 2 Apr. 2017, www.internethistorypodcast.com/2017/04/the-history-of-google/.

"The History of Google." *Internet History Podcast*, 2 Apr. 2017, www.internethistorypodcast.com/2017/04/the-history-of-google/.

"A Look at The History of Google and How It Was Founded." *ZNetLive Blog - A Guide to Domains, Web Hosting & Cloud Computing*, 30 July 2019, www.znetlive.com/blog/a-look-at-the-history-of-google-and-how-it-was-founded/.

"How We Started and Where We Are Today: Google." *About*, about.google/intl/en_us/our-story/.

Hosch, William L., and Mark Hall. "Google Inc." *Encyclopædia Britannica*,

Encyclopædia Britannica, Inc., 18 July 2019, www.britannica.com/topic/Google-Inc.

O'Connell, Brian. "History of Google: How It Began and What's Happening Beyond 2019." *TheStreet*, 31 Dec. 2018, www.thestreet.com/technology/history-of-google-14820930.

Bellis, Mary. "Google: The Story Behind One of the Richest Companies in the World." *ThoughtCo*, ThoughtCo, 18 Jan. 2019, www.thoughtco.com/who-invented-google-1991852.

Statt, Nick. "Google Is Facing an Imminent Antitrust Investigation from the US Justice Department." *The Verge*, The Verge, 1 June 2019, www.theverge.com/2019/5/31/18648052/google-us-justice-department-doj-investigation-antitrust-search.

Romm, Tony. "Google Fined Nearly $1.7 Billion for Ad Practices That E.U. Says Violated Antitrust Laws." *The Washington Post*, WP Company, 20 Mar. 2019, beta.washingtonpost.com/technology/2019/03/20/google-fined-nearly-billion-ad-practices-that-violated-european-antitrust-laws/.

Made in the USA
Monee, IL
22 November 2020